Hell Hath No Fury Like Love

Aditi Agarwal

Made with ❤ on the BookLeaf Publishing Platform
www.bookleafpub.in
www.bookleafpub.com

Dedication

To everyone whose heart has been in love and its Joy. And to all the family and friends who stood by when that heart broke.

Preface

Any powerful emotion when written down gives you the direction to feel it completely and navigate through the chaos it creates in your mind. Writing, to me, has always been a therapeutic medium to vent out and take (comparatively) sane decisions.

This book aims to reach out to all those who feel too much.

You're not alone in this journey.

Acknowledgements

This couldn't have been done without the support of my people who carry me through all kinds of chaos. You know who you are. I am eternally grateful to you.

1. Icarus

There was once a boy called Icarus
Trapped, he was determined to escape the circus.
Gathering abundant feathers relentlessly
Wax frozen wings glinted liberally.

Jumping out of the prison hesitantly
He soared high up ecstatically,
Tongue tingling with the sweet taste of liberty;
His whole being warmed up with glee
And sunrays that licked his face, chest and the wings
attached snugly.

The wax started to melt,
Threatening to snatch away this joy he felt.
Unbothered, he kept striving onwards,
Refusing to believe in the myth of gravity downwards.
Afterall this loving warmth was the beckoning of the
mighty golden star
It would protect and heal all of his scars.

Inching up towards his damnation,
Falling feathers threatened his salvation.
At last, he took a swan dive into the ocean down below
glimmering

Drowning,
Dying,
Loving.

2. Red

Red. It was her favourite colour.

It was the "colour of love" - as she called it.

It was the colour of the streak in her hair that she had adamantly gotten even after being told off by her mother multiple times,

It was the colour of the tattoo she'd gotten just above her waist,

It was the colour of the fruit she hated on her pizza,

It was the colour of the car her father had given her as her graduation present.

It was the colour of her cheeks when she talked about him,

It was the colour of the flower that he had given her in front of her favourite band,

It was the colour of her eyes when she had said yes to him.

It was the colour of her lips as she got ready,

It was the colour of the elegant gown she had donned as she traced her steps with him around that golden warmth.

It was the colour of the roses which were spread on her bed as she entered her bedroom,

Red was all she could see behind her eyes as he made love to her.

The hands of the clock raced in a blur and...
Red was the colour of her lips as a liquid of the same
colour oozed out of her lips,
It was the colour of her cheek in the shape of a human
hand,
It was the colour of her eyes as she shielded her face
from him.
But black was the colour of the skin around her eyes,
And blue was the colour of the five small circles around
her arms,
And pink was the colour of the finger which he pointed
at her while threatening her to do as he says or he would
harm her family,
And white was the colour of the floor to which she
looked at while nodding her head.

The race continued and...
Red was the colour of the warm food she had prepared
for him as it was their anniversary,
Red was the colour of her eyes as she fought sleep
waiting for him to come home;
It was the colour of the saree she started dreaming about
him gifting her.

And red was the colour of his face as he saw her sound
asleep in the chair next to cold food,

It was the colour of the wine bottle that was sitting on
the table
Which he picked up and raised above his head.

Red was now the colour of the chair and the floor on
which she now laid, quite pale.
It was the colour of the letters on the windshield of the
white vehicle that carried her.

But white was the colour her family wore the next day,
And red was the colour another girl wore as she sat next
to him
With red smeared in her hairline – The symbol of love.

3. Altar

I close my eyes as my lips move to form a silent prayer
I close my eyes as my lips lay over yours...

I bow down my head in front of God
End up worshipping at your altar.

Loving you, worshipping Him - What's the difference!?

4. Caught in a crossfire

Cherry blossoms
Thick milkshakes
Soft white snow
Sunny afternoons
Sitting in the shade of a tree
Thick green moss;
Dark woods
Pitch black bottom of well
Demons howling in my ears
An abandoned midnight highway
Being trapped in a pitch black bat cave.

Smell of freshly brewed coffee
Whiff from a new novel
Wind through my hair
Walking along the beach
Soft yellow lit streets;
Dark alleys
Long shadows
Long thin fingers gripping my throat
A lonely wolf howling nearby.

Warm water in bathtub
With scented candles and tealights

Christmas carols and old songs
Swinging in a hammock on a beach;
A brand new car wrecked
A dagger twisting through my heart
Missing you.

Raindrops on my face
Rainbows over mountains;
Loving you.

-    How the pendulum swings in the endless timeline of
me loving you.

5. Forever Young

There was once a boy who wanted to stay young forever.
He swore to himself that he'd find a way by the time he's
25 and stay that age until his time comes.
Science, astrology, dark magic - he explored everything
you could possibly name - with no success.

Until one day,
When he was 24 years and 3 days old;
A supernova exploded and there landed a part of
sunshine brighter than the sun itself in front him,
illuminating every nano-crook inside him.
He forgot what he was so ardently looking for.

He'd heard about such explosions from other people
before
But he always disregarded them because
Duh! He was too smart to believe that something so
much greater than himself could exist.
Until now.
And like all great romances, this too came to an end.
And like all smart people do, he moved on.

Today, at the age of 28, ask him what he had for
breakfast

And he'd tell you he doesn't bother with such lame
details.
But ask him what he had for dinner on Christmas 4 years
ago
And he'd give you a detailed narrative of those 3 hours
as if it were yesterday,
Including how many times the wind had blown her hair.

 Sometimes wishes do come true.

Just not in the form you hope for.

6. Of Time and its Beauty

Time o time, you beautiful bastard!
How are you so graceful and yet so brutal
So calming but suddenly tempestuous;
Healing up wounds which were once incurable
Yet cutting so deep at the mere stroke of a feather.

Like some music flowing out through ancient ages
Which enlightens the soul and stabilises the mind;
That awakens the sleepy nymphs and naiads
And fills the air with an eternal mirth.

You have a way of turning things around in directions
unfathomable
Towards people unimaginable
And places humanly unreachable.

The way you paint our lives
Second by second, without a touch
Leaving the once gloomy, grey canvas
Splashed with fine strokes and bold hues;
Testifies the age old adage -
"Everything sorts out in the end
And if it hasn't, it's not the end".

7. Love at First Sight

Brown.
It has always been a boring colour to me honestly.
It always reminds me of gritty dirt, decaying things and
cowdung. In fact, I didn't even own a dress in brown.
I could never fathom someone even remotely liking the
colour.
What could possibly have gone wrong with someone to
have their favorite colour as brown! Ughhh!!!
The only thing I liked (and loved) of its shade was
chocolate. Duh!
But then it was a different colour to me. Chocolate
brown, I used to call it. I had grown up with the same
unwavering feeling towards the colour, until the day I
saw them.

The two brown circular heavenly bodies set in brilliant
white globes placed in the upper part of his head.
That one moment melted away my 19 years of constant
dislike and created a warm yearning for brown as if it
was the one thing that has kept me anchored to this
earth all along.
Earth.
Ohh the smell of the earth after it rains! That's how you
made me feel.

Alive and intoxicated.
Oh boy! Earth is brown too.
How did I never see the homely compassion this colour
offers!

I stood still as my world spinned round.
You came towards me.
My heart beating louder than ever with every step you
took. I was worried if you came any closer you might
hear what I already could.
Thankfully you stopped midway, put your hand on the
table - oh that brown lucky bastard - and with the other
hand you picked up the coffee mug.
Coffee! But I LOVE coffee. You were brown all along too!
It was as if everything was dawning on me at once.

The world seemed so new to me that I started doubting if
I ever actually walked with eyes open.
You lingered on for a while, your eyelids hiding them
from me like clouds sneak up on the moon at night.

And in that moment, I turned around and ran.
I ran as fast as I could into nothing; to preserve this
moment forever in my heart.
Coz I don't know what would've happened when you
looked up.
I would find that out tomorrow.

But today, for now, this moment was perfect and nothing was going to taint that.

It was only mine to keep.

Just mine.

8. Sandcastles

I once built a sandcastle at my favourite beach. It was my prettiest creation yet. Adorned with flowers and pebbles and careful strokes.
I ran to proudly show it off to my friends.
By the time we came back, the sea had engulfed it.
I mourned it for a whole hour swearing not to ever build one ever again. Only coming back next week to do the same.

Happily, hopefully.

I wish we'd give our hearts the same liberty.
To get broken and have enough faith and courage to mend what we didn't break.

And maybe create the best damn sandcastle ever.

Until the next wave.

9. Gods' Plan

The broken wing of a warrior
An ocean of disappointment and loss,
Eyes wandered for a bleak ray of hope
As the ruins of her own destruction lay at her feet.

Thundering through the grayest clouds
Descends an angel with a smile brighter than the sun;
Stretching out his flawless palm
There lay the most beautiful medallion she ever saw.

She looks at him, eyes brimming with questions
His lips stretch over his perfect teeth
A lightening bolt runs through her heart
His brown eyes hold hers earnestly
As the most beautiful sound the Gods ever created
escapes his throat -
"It's yours, of course! You brave little warrior."

The destruction at her feet shivers
She waits for him to laugh in mockery
But the angel continues to smile
And before her mind could form a comprehensive
thought
The distance in between turned naught

His fingers busy adorning the new owner of the
medallion.

The rubble at her feet growls
Rising up, rearranging itself
Forming the most beautiful landscape
Then landing softly near her feet.

Her mind whispered through the thick happy fog her
heart was creating
"Careful, child. All good things come tethered to an
unseen misery."
But the wings of the little bird beating in her chest
Tired of the unyielding weight of hopelessness
Was glad to have the chance to fly again.

A mischievous glint crossed the angel's eyes
As they reflected the pure happiness in the broken
warrior's face
An uneasy feeling crossed her mind;
"You're very perceptive, my little one", he utters in a
sultry voice.
"Is there more to you than meets the eye, my lord?"

The warm brown in his eyes turns to cold black
His lips curl to form an empty smile
"Why yes my child, for you see

I'm not just another angel.
I'm the greatest one.
I'm Lucifer.
Take care, my brave one.
And Always Expect Miracles."

And with that the fallen angel turns away,
Leaving the warrior lost in a myriad of questions and
emotions.

Who knows why the Gods do what they do.

10. Apple of my Eyes

"An apple a day keeps a doctor away," they said.
I've never been a fan of apples though honestly.

And then that one fine day you happened.

I was sitting in my usual corner immersed in reading yet
another mystery when you broke my reverie. Those two
letters wrapped in one simple, totally commonplace
word and yet it seemed so foreign altogether I felt an
urge to investigate the unearthly origin of that "hi".

I looked up hungrily to attach a face to that silky yet
husky voice. A sound which I can't attach any right
adjective to. I stood up in a manner I was hoping was
confident. You asked me for directions to some place that
was not my heart and as you spoke the bulge in the
centre of your neck was dancing.
Such a beautiful creation.

That was the time I fell in love with the apples.
Or to be precise, your Adam's apple.

11. Pangea

Tectonic shifts and quaking earth,
Beautiful peaks and deepest valleys.
Gush of ocean in a once arid desert,
Blooming flowers and lush mangroves
Where happiness was once a mirage.

Some disasters are just waiting to happen
Waiting to unearth heaven.

12. Of Art and Healing

So it's a lazy Sunday afternoon and I'm lazing on the bed
with a book in my hand. He's lying on the other side of
the bed, snoring after having scrolled through his
newsfeed multiple times, bored.
It's his soft snores that make me look up from that
thrilling plot. I watch his chest heave up and down with
each breath he takes.
His face is tilted towards his left and the bead of
Rudraksh he wears on a red thread is almost visible
making a slight bulge through the white t-shirt he's
wearing, also shifted to the same side. His hair is ruffled.
Not the usual perfect gel set kind that he always
portrays, but rather the out of place messy kind you read
about in books that makes your heart skip a beat.
His lips are slightly ajar. He's breathing through his
mouth again. I can now see a small ball of saliva forming
in the edge, ready to trickle out as soon as some more
balls come and join it. The sun streams through the
window falling on his face, lighting it up and
accentuating the creases forming on his forehead.
Next to him lies the notebook in which he diligently
scribbles his heart out in the form of most beautiful and
heartbreaking poems you'll ever read whenever he's sad,
pining for that girl.

That girl who is his one true love.
The one who comes to his mind just before falling asleep
and the one whose memories don't let him sleep.
The one he talks to his best friends about.
The one whose heart he'd broken.
The one who loved him in all the clichéd ways possible.
The one he regrets letting go.
The one that he was now sure was "The One."

I watch him and think to myself - Why is it that we
choose the people that we can't have?
Him pining after her, me pining after him... It's a vicious
cycle.
But it is the one that keeps most of the writers going.

So when we get our hearts broken and bleed it out on a
paper, we create art.
And when that art finds its way to someone else's heart,
maybe it will heal them.
And maybe even us.

Maybe.

13. Gray

The sun streamed through the window
Lighting up the room and a half of your face
In that moment I realised what you are
A perfect amalgamation of light and dark.

You looked beautiful that day
And you were all mine to keep.
Both the good and the bad parts,
All mine.

14. Too Good To Be True!!!

It was just another summer day
Dull and boring – I was about to doze away,
Just then you entered through the door
Carrying along a gust of wind offshore;
My eyes locked with you
Like a paper to the glue
Babe! You were just too good to be true.

Chaos reigned and cupid's arrows clamoured
You were a knight in the shining armour,
So high on your steed
Almost beyond my reach;
Like a holy grail to be pursued
You seemed like an elusive muse
Coz babe! You were too good to be true.

Fate conspired, destiny rewired
My heart fluttered faster than it was hardwired,
The impossible crawled towards the plausible
And the stars suddenly became feasible;
You were no longer a stranger out of the blue
Rather, an old friend my heart always knew
But, my love, you were just too good to be true.

You amazed me with all your wits
Especially your laugh, it blew my mind to bits
There was something quite addictive about you
Maybe that I could be 'me' around you;
And just as you'd started evolving
Into the picture of "my human being",
A raven cried, my eyes fluttered open wide
Realization dawned upon my groggy mind
And I registered the familiar room...

Yes, my love, you were too good to be true.

15. First Kiss

5 seconds when I forgot how to breathe
5 seconds when you took the leap
5 seconds when your lips were on mine
12 heart beats as intoxicating as wine
5 seconds of utter bliss
5 seconds when I melted in your kiss
3 seconds when my body froze
2 seconds when I pulled you close
5 seconds is all that's on my mind

The 5 seconds when you were mine.

16. Erised

I stand in front of the mirror and watch the reflection of two people - he and I.

I'm looking out at nothing in particular, trying to gather my thoughts and he is staring at me with eyes so soft, as if the phrase 'puppy dog eyes' originated from his.

Was it love?

Was it desire?

Was it the surreality of this moment?

I didn't know.

You see I have bad eyesight. I'm not good at reading people.

I'm a person who falls for words.

So when I finally look back at him and he tells me he loves this moment, I believe him.

When he tells me he's never going to forget us, I trust him.

When he closes the space between us and seals my lips with a kiss, I fall for him.

When he takes my hand in his and says he never wants to let it go; I melt into his arms, him.

A tear falls down my cheek as I look down at my own empty hands which are outstretched as they ache to find

his. Instead, they land on an inscription above the mirror.
It was 'desire' in his eyes after all, I guess.
Maybe that's why the mirror is called 'desire' spelled
backwards.

I chuckle as a fresh crop of tears flow down my cheeks. I
don't wipe them away.
Instead, I fall to the floor, put my chin on my knees and
watch him kiss me.

Again.

17. Questions

Do you know what do, when closely placed,
A regular and a laterally inverted question marks make?

A Heart.

My questions amalgamating with yours
To eventually find the answer.

In our love.

18. Flame of Hope

Turmoil seized her in darkness
The vile vines clawed around her throat
She rolled herself into a ball,
To protect that little flame of hope.

Medusa caressed her incessantly.
Tempting her to open her eyes
And drink on that intoxicating hatred.

But she knew if she looked into her eyes
That little flame would freeze forever.
She continued to resist
And walked blindly, headlong into whatever came next.
No, she won't melt to that incessant cooing
She had known too much happiness to believe that
demons exist.

Now the devil changed course
Unable to pry open her eyes and possess her
He aimed for the place he was sure that light came from.
Stretching a claw, he pried out her heart
And felt a foreign emotion creeping up on him.
"Fear", he recognized.
 Eyes wide open, he looked up to her.

For the first time, she was smiling
For the flame of hope didn't sit in her anatomical heart,
But danced in the core of her being
Where a crown sat adorning it.

19. A Sunny Affair

The door creaked as I pulled it apart a few inches
To taste the sunrays, defying all my instincts;
The sun felt warm soaking deep into my pores
As if my soul sailing offshore;
But the ecstasy took me a little bit too far
And all I was left with was a sunburn and scar.

20. Be Careful What You Wish for

I close my eyes and take a deep breath
Blow on the fluffy white dandelion
Whisper into the air what my heart ardently desired -
Love - a passion that consumes your whole being
Yet leaves you ecstatic and unscathed
Always wanting more.

The seeds soar to the wishing well
A star shoots across the sky,
Droplets rain down like metaphorical arrows
As my eyes navigate the storm to find their harbour in
yours.

Little did I know,
Cupid died and left Satan in charge.

I fell,
You didn't.

21. Sunshine

Class : 7

Subject : Science

"Plants need sunlight to grow and survive."

When I called you my sunshine,
I meant exactly that.

Do you know what happens to flowers
Without their sunshine?

22. Last Slice

Tangled limbs,
Heavy breaths and
Locked eyes.
Hands outstretched
Holding the last pizza slice.

Waiting for the other
To give in,
He put an end in his mouth
Closed the distance in between
Offering her the other end of the slice.

Their kisses had never tasted better than this.

23. Parallel Universe

"Hey babe!"

I call out loudly from the other side of the room
As easily as I breathe.
You come and stand behind me
Close enough for me to feel the heat emanating from
your body
And my body still tingles after such a long time.

You lean down to whisper in my ear -
"You need something?"
And my insides squeeze at
The low hush tone of your voice
And I close my eyes as your breath
Hits my ear and its smell fills my lungs.

I see white and light blue instead of
The usual red behind my eyes
Because nothing is ever rooted
In this commonplace world with you.
You instantly transport me to my happiest place.

A breeze flows across my face as you put
Your left arm around me

And put those sweet soft lips on my neck.

"I love you",
I say almost like a gasp
Mustering whatever air I could.
Not as a confession
But as a thank you to the God above.
"I know, silly!"
You mumble into my skin.

In a parallel universe this is happening
I tell myself as I fall asleep
After a fitful few hours of
Anxiety and melancholy.

Because in any other universe,
You'd know.

24. Happy accidents

Walking down the hall
Absent minded
Crashing into you
Blind sided.

Books fall down
Pages come apart
You stoop down
And pick up my heart.

25. Your Name

"J" - thud - thud – thud – /butterflies/
*Lo*cked eyes, long sighs
Feather touches, warm blushes
Stolen stares, hitched breaths
Coy smiles, finest dines
First kisses, shooting star wishes.
I wish this would never end.

"J" – thud – thud - /waves of love/ - thud – thud - /waves
of bliss/
Mellow eyes, sleepy sighs
Familiar touches, halted rushes
Smitten stares, quiet breaths
Wide smiles, meals homecooked style
Mirthful kisses, granted wishes.
Promise me, this is forever.

"J" - thud – thud – thud – thud – /storm/ - thud – thud –
thud – thud - /stampede/
Damp eyes, deafening cries
Craving touches, loud hushes
Empty stares, shallow breaths
Banished smile, tongue drowning in bile
Familial kisses, broken wishes.

When will all this end?

Spring melts into winter, summer a blur
A ray of sunshine manages to traverse
The frozen icicles biting into her heart disperse,
The ray rushes to warm her whole being
And hushes the raging battles within.
It forges a blade so sharp
Destroying anything moulding her self-worth warped ,
This ray of love that she harbours for herself
Refused to yield to any monster from hell.
Henceforth rose the bright red wings
From the ashes with fortified heart strings,
Sprinkling the air with the sweetest melody
Infusing merriment and dispelling maladies.

"J" – thud – /Calm/.

26. अल्प लम्हें

कुछ अधूरी सी गुफ्तगू,
कुछ बोलती खामोशियाँ
कुछ फूलों सा खिलखिला देना तेरा,
कुछ आँखों का झील हो जाना मेरा;
कुछ बिखरी जुलफें मेरी,
कुछ संवारती उंगलियाँ तेरी
कुछ आसमान छू लेना साथ तेरे,
कुछ पाताल के नीचे पहुँच जाना बिन तेरे;
कुछ मेरी खाली हथेलियों का रह रह के सिमटना,
कुछ तेरा ना होके भी साँस साँस होना
कुछ यूँहीं गुम हो जाना मेरा,
कुछ मुझको फिर से ढूंढ लाना तेरा;
कुछ तेरा कुछ भी ना होना,
कुछ तेरा सबकुछ हो जाना।

27. ज़रूरतें

कहते है रोज़ किसी चीज़ को देखो तो
उसकी अहमियत कम हो जाती है,
उसके होने का सच
उसके गुम होने के डर को धुंधला देता है।

कहते है रोज़ कोई काम करो तो
उसकी आदत हो जाती है
और आदतों का क्या है
एक बार लगी तो छूटने में
इक अर्सा लग जाता है।

मैं अक्सर सोचती थी
तुम दूसरी श्रेणी में आते हो
आदत हो,
एक दिन छूट ही जाओगे।
फ़िर एक दिन उस चाँद ने पूछा
"क्या मैं भी आदत हूँ तुम्हारी?"

मैने नज़रें झुका ली।

कुछ चीज़े आदत नहीं
जीने का ज़रिया होती है,
जैसे साँसें लेना
बारिश की बूंदों को हथेलियों में समेटना

आसमान में बादलों को ताकना
समंदर की लहरों की अठखेलियाँ सुनना

तुम्हें याद करना।

28. काश

धुँधली यादें, धुँधली बातें
धुंधली तसवीरें, धुंधले वादें
कुछ इनही में बसर होती जा रही है
ये रफ़्तार से बढ़ती हुई जिंदगी।
काश कभी यूं हो के वक्त थमे
और सिर्फ तुम और मैं हो
इस दुनिया से अलग
इन धुंधली यादों को कुछ साफ करे
थोड़ा फिर तुम अपनी उंगलियों से
मेरी हथेली को सहलाओ
थोड़ा मैं फिर से मोम सी पिघल जाऊँ
थोड़े फिर से धुँधले हो
वो शीशें जिनपे सांसें तेरी मेहरबान हो
थोड़ी फिर से धुँधला जाएँ
मेरी आँखें जो तेरे जाने की बात हो।
थोड़ा तू फिर से मुस्कुराए,
अपने होठों से मेरे होठों को सहलाए
थोड़ा मेरी धड़कनें तेरी धड़कनों से गुप्तगु करे
थोड़ा मैं तेरी बाहों में,
तुझ में समा जाऊ।

29. अमावस

आज फिर वही शाम आई
चाँद फिर बादलों से झाक रहा था
आज फिर मेरे दिल ने तुम्हे पुकारा
वो मोर भी आज शायद सुन रहा था
पूँछा, "आज इतने दिनों बाद तुझे फिर कैसे याद आई?"
मैंने हँस के फिर आसमान की ओर नज़र घुमाई
"अमावस की रात ये चाँद भी तो नहीं दिखता
छुपा होता है, गायब नहीं।"

30. ख़्वाहिश

एक लम्हा तेरी यादों का
एक टुकड़ा तेरे आसमान के चांद की चांदनी का
एक पल तेरी हंसी की खनक का
एक टुकड़ा तेरे माथे पर पड़ती लकीरों का
एक अहसास मेरे हाथ में तेरी हथेली का
एक रुकी सांस तेरे होठों से मेरे नाम सुन्ना
एक खुशबु तेरी सांसो की
एक किस्सा तेरे उन दोस्तों का
एक सिलसिला तेरी शरारतों का
एक मौका तेरी आंखों से खुद को देखने का
एक महफ़िल तेरी बातों की, तेरी मरहम सी आवाज़ की
एक पल तेरा जाने के लिए कदम बढ़ाना
एक पल मेरा बस दो मिनट कहके तुझे आखिरी बार रोकना

और
एक पल तेरी धड़कन के एहसास का

और..
और एक पल..

खैर छोड़ो।